Learning F

Learn React JS From Scratch v

2nd Edition

2020

By Claudia Alves

For information contact :

(alabamamond@gmail.com, memlnc)

http://www.memlnc.com

2nd Edition: 2020

Learning React js

"Programming isn't about what you know; it's about what you can figure out." - *Chris Pine*

Before you begin, please note that this is a beginner-friendly guide that covers the concepts I classify as fundamentals for working with React. It is not a complete guide to React but rather a complete introduction.

At the end of this guide, I list a few next-level resources for you. This guide will pave the way for you to understand them.

Content

Introduction

Facebook's React has changed the way we think about web applications and user interface development. Due to its design, you can use it beyond web. A feature known as the Virtual DOM enables this.

In this chapter we'll go through some of the basic ideas behind the library so you understand React a little better before moving on.

What is React?

React is a JavaScript library that forces you to think in terms of components. This model of thinking fits user interfaces well. Depending on your background it might feel alien at first. You will have to think very carefully about the concept of state and where it belongs.

Because state management is a difficult problem, a variety of solutions have appeared. In this book, we'll start by managing state ourselves and then push it to a Flux implementation known as Alt. There are also implementations available for several other alternatives, such as Redux, MobX, and Cerebral.

React is pragmatic in the sense that it contains a set of escape hatches. If the React model doesn't work for you, it is still possible to revert back to something lower level. For instance, there are hooks that can be used to wrap older logic that relies on the DOM. This breaks the abstraction and ties your code to a specific environment, but sometimes that's the pragmatic thing to do.

One of the fundamental problems of programming is how to deal with state. Suppose you are developing a user interface and want to show the same data in multiple places. How do you make sure the data is consistent?

Historically we have mixed the concerns of the DOM and state and tried to manage it there. React solves this problem in a different way. It introduced the concept of the **Virtual DOM** to the masses.

Virtual DOM exists on top of the actual DOM, or some other render target. It solves the state manipulation problem in its own way. Whenever changes are made to it, it figures out the best way to batch the changes to the underlying DOM structure. It is able to propagate changes across its virtual tree as in the image above.

Virtual DOM Performance

Handling the DOM manipulation this way can lead to increased performance. Manipulating the DOM by hand tends to be inefficient and is hard to optimize. By leaving the problem of DOM manipulation to a good implementation, you can save a lot of time and effort.

React allows you to tune performance further by implementing hooks to adjust the way the virtual tree is updated. Though this is often an optional step.

The biggest cost of Virtual DOM is that the implementation makes React quite big. You can expect the bundle sizes of small applications to be around 150-200 kB minified, React included. gzipping will help, but it's still big.

React facilitates the creation of interactive user interfaces. Just design views for each status in your app, and React will efficiently update and synthesize the right components when your data changes.

React relies primarily on the concept of components. You have to build packaged components that manage their own state, and then install these components together to create complex user interfaces. Since component logic is written using JavaScript instead of template mode, you can easily pass a lot of data through your application and keep the state away from DOM.

React is based on the principle of "learning once and writing anywhere". You don't assume you are dealing with a specific technology, but you can develop new features without rewriting a new code. React can be rendered on the server using Node.js, and mobile applications can be created via React Native.

Terminology in React

Single-page app

Single-page Application is an application that loads a single HTML page and all the necessary extensions (such as CSS and JavaScript) required for the application to work. No interactions with the page or subsequent pages require a return to the server again, which means that the page is not reloaded.

Although you can build a single-page application in React, it is not necessary. React can also be used to optimize small portions of the site with greater interactivity. A code written using React can co-exist with the format on the server using PHP or any other server-side libraries. In fact, this is exactly how to use React on Facebook.

ES6, ES2015, ES2016, etc ..

These abbreviations refer to the latest versions of the ECMAScript standard, for which JavaScript is implemented. ES6 (also called ES2015) includes many additions to earlier versions such as arrow functions, classes, literal templates, and let and const statements. You can learn more about the specific versions here.

Banks

The JavaScript sink takes JavaScript code, converts it, and returns JavaScript in another format. The most common use case is to take the ES6 wording and convert it to an older wording so that older browsers can interpret it. The most frequently used banker with React is Babel.

Bundlers

Packers take CSS and JavaScript code written as separate modules (usually hundreds), and group them together in a few performance-optimized files for browsers. One of the most commonly used packages in React applications is Webpack and Browserify.

Package Manager

Package Manager is a tool that allows you to manage the credits in your project. The two most commonly used packet managers in React are npm and Yarn, both of which are the interface of the same npm packet recorder.

Content Distribution Network

CDN stands for Content Delivery Network. These networks distribute static and cached content from a network of servers around the world.

JSX

JSX is an extended formatting to JavaScript, which is similar to template language but has the full power of JavaScript. JSX behaves into calls to the React.createElement () function, which returns abstract JavaScript objects called React elements. For an introduction to JSX see here, and for more detailed information about JSX see here.

React DOM uses the camelCase naming convention instead of the HTML property names. For example, the tabindex property becomes tabIndex in JSX. The class property is also written as className because class is a reserved word in JavaScript:

```
const name = 'Clementine';

ReactDOM.render (

<h1 className = "hello"> My name is {name}! </h1>,

document.getElementById ('root')

);
```

Elements

React elements are modules for building React applications. One might confuse elements with a more common concept of components. The item describes what you want to see on the screen, and the React elements are not editable:

```
const element = <h1> Hello world </h1>;
```

Items are not usually used directly, but are returned from components.

the ingredients

React components are small, reusable pieces of code that return the React elements to be rendered on the page. The simplest form of the React component is an abstract JavaScript function that returns the React element:

```
function Welcome (props) {

return <h1> Hi {props.name} </h1>;

}
```

Components of ES6 varieties may also be:

```
class Welcome extends React.Component {

render () {

return <h1> Hi {this.props.name} </h1>;

}

}
```

Components can be divided into functionally independent parts that can be used among other components. Components can return other components, arrays, text strings, and numbers. The rule here is that if part of your user interface is used multiple times (such as buttons, control panel and avatar), or if it is complex (application, comment), it is a good candidate to be a reusable component. Component names must always begin with a capital letter (<Wrapper />, not <wrapper />). .

Characteristics

Props are inputs into the React components, that is, data passed to the lower level of the parent component to the son component.

Remember that the properties are read-only and should not be modified in any way:

// Error!

props.number = 42;

If you need to modify some values in response to user input or responses from the network, use the state instead.

props.children

Props.children is available in each component and contains content between the opening tag and the closing tag of the component, for example:

<Welcome> Hello world! </Welcome>

The text string is "Hello world!" Available under props.children in the Welcome component:

```
function Welcome (props) {

return <p> {props.children} </p>;

}
```

For components defined as classes, use this.props.children:

```
class Welcome extends React.Component {

render () {

return <p> {this.props.children} </p>;

}

}
```

Case

The component needs state when some of the data associated with it changes over time. For example, the Checkbox component needs to have isChecked in its state, and the NewsFeed component needs to track all fetchedPosts in its state.

The biggest difference between the state and the properties is that the properties are passed from the parent component, and the state is managed by the component itself. The component cannot change its properties but can change its status. To do this he must call the child this.setState (). Only components defined as classes can have a status.

For each specific piece of variable data, there must be one component that it owns in its state. Don't try to sync statuses to two different components, instead elevate the status to their nearest shared parent and pass it to lower levels as attributes for both.

Life cycle dependencies

Lifecycle dependencies are a custom function performed during different phases of component life. Dependents are available when the component is created and inserted into the DOM, when the component is updated, and when the component is removed or removed from the DOM.

Adjusted and unconfigured components

React has two different methods when working with input fields.

The input field element whose value is set by React is called the justified component. When the user enters the data into the configured component, a change event handler is fired and your code determines whether the entries are valid (by rendering with the updated value). If you do not reset, the input field element remains unchanged.

The unset component works the same way as field items outside React. When a user enters data into an input field (such as an input field box or a drop-down list), the new information is reversed without React having to do anything. This means that you cannot force fields to have specific values.

In most cases you should use the configured component.

Keys

A key is a attribute and a text string that you need to include when creating elements from arrays. The React keys help identify elements that have been changed, added, or removed. Keys must be given to the elements inside an array to give the elements a stable identity.

Keys must be unique only within sibling elements of the same matrix; they should not be unique throughout the application or even in a single component.

Don't pass something like Math.random () to the keys. It is important that the keys have stable identities during rendering so that React can determine when to add, remove, or rearrange items. Keys must match stable and unique identifiers coming from your data, such as post.id.

References

React supports a unique feature that you can link to any component. The ref property can be a component arising from the React.createRef () function, a callback function, or a text string (in the old API). When the ref property is a call function, the function will receive the corresponding DOM element or a copy of the class (depending on the type of element) as its argument. This allows direct access to the DOM element or component instance.

Use references with caution. If you find yourself using it a lot to do things in your app, consider whether you can adapt to top-down data flow.

Events

Event handling in React elements has some wording differences:

React event handlers are called camelCase instead of lowercase letters.

In JSX, it passes the function as an event handler instead of passing a text string.

Matching

When the status or properties of the component change, React determines whether a DOM update is necessary by comparing the newly restored element with the previous creator. When they are not equal, React updates the DOM model. This process is called reconciliation.

Consulting and paid services

Since 2016, I am happy to do 1 on 1 consulting, search problems in the code, help in preparing for an interview, etc. Good baggage of experience,
which I am ready to share in understandable language.

Connecting react'a using a tag script

React.js is just a library. Not a framework.

Like any other library, a react is added to the page using the tag
script .

Since in modern js modules and various kinds of transformations /
contractions "rule"
and so on - *react is* great with *webpack* , *babel* and others. For
simplicity, we
let's start working with react like a regular library like jQuery, but
then
let's move on to a convenient tool - create-react-app .
Create the following files in your project directory.
+ - .gitignore (if using git)
+ - index.html

index.html

In the programming world, every lesson starts with hello, world.
index.html

```
<! DOCTYPE html>
<html>
<head>
<meta charset = "UTF-8" />
<title> React [RU] Tutorial </title>
<script src = "https://unpkg.com/react@16/umd/react.development.js" >
</script>
<script src = "https://unpkg.com/react-dom@16/umd/react-
dom.development.js" > </script>
<! - Don't use this in production ->
<script src = "https://unpkg.com/babel-standalone@6.15.0/babel.min.js" >
</script>
</head>
<body>
<div id = "root" > </div>
<script type = "text / babel" >
</script>
</body>
</html>
```

First, we connected the react and react-dom libraries as regular
scripts
Secondly, we have included the babel library so that our line
<h1> Hello world! </h1>,
which is written in the helper JSX language has become valid
javascript-
the code:

React.createElement ("h1", null, "Hello, world!"),

We will be using JSX throughout the tutorial.

Component creation

ReactDOM.render accepts a react component (hereinafter I will simply call
"component") and the DOM element into which we want to "mount" our
attachment.

<h1> Hello, world! </h1> - oddly enough, this is a primitive component.
Nothing exciting yet, but let's imagine this pseudo code:

```
var photos = [ 'images / cat.jpg' , 'images / dog.jpg' , 'images / owl.jpg' ]
ReactDOM.render (
<App>
<Photos photos = photos />
<LastNews />
<Comments />
</App>,
document.getElementById ('root')
);
```

What is remarkable about this pseudo-code? It reads very well, because
it is obvious that our application (App) displays: photo (cat, dog, owl),
news and comments.
I want to please you, the React.js code looks almost the same. It reads perfectly,
since the division into components allows you to perfectly structure the code.
Let's create a primitive component:
index.html

```
<! DOCTYPE html>
...
<body>
<div id = "root"> </div>
<script type = "text / babel">
const App = () => {
return <p> Hello everyone, I'm an App component </p>
}
ReactDOM.render (
<App />,
```

```
document.getElementById ('root')
);
</script>
</body>
</html>
```

What is remarkable? We hid the markup in `<App />` . Yes, in this example it is one
the line and the feeling of euphoria is absent, but it will still be! For now, remember that if
we want to render the component in JSX, then we must definitely name and
cause it to **Big** letters.
Let's look at the resulting html code:
We created a component using a function. But components can be created with
using `class` . Let's kill several birds with one stone:
learn how to create components using class
how to pass css style
how to render multiple components at once
index.html

```
<! DOCTYPE html>
<html>
<head>
<meta charset = "UTF-8" />
<title> React [RU] Tutorial v2 </title>
<script src = "https://unpkg.com/react@16/umd/react.development.js">
</script>
<script src = "https://unpkg.com/react-dom@16/umd/react-
dom.development.js"> </ script
>
<script src = "https://unpkg.com/babel-standalone@6.15.0/babel.min.js">
</script>
<style>
.red {
color: # FF0000;
}
</style>
</head>
<body>
<div id = "root"> </div>
<script type = "text / babel">
const App = () => {
return <p> Hello everyone, I'm an App component </p>
}
class BigApp extends React.Component {
```

```
render () {
return (
<div>
<h1> I am a component, BigApp </h1>
<p className = 'red'> Components can be nested within each other. </p>
<App />
</div>
)
}
}
ReactDOM.render (
<BigApp />,
document.getElementById ('root')
);
</script>
</body>
</html>
```

Syntax:

class (name) extends (what we will inherit)

also allows you to create a component. It is worth noting here that if the component is created

using a class, the JSX markup is written inside the **render** method . This is key

a method in which we specify what will be displayed to the user on the page.

Components created with a class are called statefull components (that is,

components with *state*), and components created with a function are stateless

component (that is, *stateless* components). Why such a division - we will find out later.

In the example, we added the style for the paragraph, through className , and not through class , like

we are used to doing this. Why? Because we are inside the JSX syntax,

where html and js are mixed, and the word class is reserved in javascript.

Finally, I note that we were able to easily nest one component into another.

In the markup, everything is as we expected. However, I already see readers who don't like

extra div .

Each component should return one
knot

Consider the div problem. As the title says, we must return always one dom node. Let's try to remove the div:
index.html

```
<script type = "text / babel">
const App = () => {
return <p> Hello everyone, I'm an App component </p>
}
class BigApp extends React.Component {
render () {
// removed the div
return (
<h1> I am a component, BigApp </h1>
<p className = 'red'> Components can be nested within each other. </p>
<App />
)
}
}
ReactDOM.render (
<BigApp />,
document.getElementById ('root')
);
</script>
```

Error: jsx elements must be wrapped in one tag. What to do if you don't feel like it
fence another div? Answer: React.Fragment
Everyone is happy. There is not much difference, as you like better, write this way, but
remember: everything that you return in the render method or in the return of the stateless component
must be wrapped in a single tag / React.Fragment.
Let's develop an idea: teach BigApp to display news. For this, we you will need to create a <News /> component and nest it in BigApp.
index.html

```
const App = () => {
return <p> Hello everyone, I'm an App component </p>
}
```

```
const News = () => {
return <p> Sorry, no news </p>
}
class BigApp extends React . Component {
render () {
return (
<React.Fragment>
<h1> I am a component, BigApp </h1>
<p className = 'red'> Components can be nested within each other. </p>
<App />
<News />
</React.Fragment>
)
}
}
ReactDOM.render (
<BigApp />,
document.getElementById ('root')
);
```

Let's take a look at the code again and look for interesting places.

First , we haven't changed the code inside ReactDOM.render in any way. We just invested

BigApp has another component.

Secondly , as already mentioned, the <BigApp /> component contains a component

<News /> as if it were just a child of a <div> </div> element.

Third , our <News /> component is as primitive as App, so we created it through a function (not through a class).

Understanding what is going on: Remove the <BigApp /> component , leave the <App

/> (without rewriting it into a statefull component). In <App />, display <News /> . So

create a <Comments /> component and make it appear after news. Component text: "No news - nothing to comment."

The solution to the problem is always published below in the text, and usually contains

hints first, and then the code of the whole solution. There are no clues here.

Solution :

index.html
```
<! DOCTYPE html>
<html>
<head>
<meta charset = "UTF-8" />
```

```html
<title> React [RU] Tutorial v2 </title>
<script src = "https://unpkg.com/react@16/umd/react.development.js">
</script>
<script src = "https://unpkg.com/react-dom@16/umd/react-
dom.development.js"> </ script
>
<script src = "https://unpkg.com/babel-standalone@6.15.0/babel.min.js">
</script>
<style>
.red {
color: # FF0000;
}
</style>
</head>
<body>
<div id = "root"> </div>
<script type = "text / babel">
const News = () => {
return <p> Sorry, no news </p>
}
const Comments = () => {
return <p> No news - nothing to comment. </p>
}
const App = () => {
return (
<React.Fragment>
<News />
<Comments />
</React.Fragment>
)
}
ReactDOM.render (
<App />,
document.getElementById ('root')
);
</script>
</body>
</html>
```

Before moving on to the next tutorial, I suggest you install react devtools
(plugin for chrome, plugin for mozilla).
Since we are developing simply in the index.html file, we need to activate the option in
plugin (looks like this in chrome):
Once installed and configured, open the React tab in the developer console.

An inquisitive reader has already noticed the "Props" window. Ok, we'll talk about this in
next chapter.
Source code at the moment.

Using props

Each component can have properties. They are stored in this.props and passed to
component as attributes.
General form:

```
const wizard = {name: Garry, surname: Potter};
<MyComponent data = {wizard} eshe_odno_svoistvo = {[1,2,3,4,5]} />
```

Any javascript primitive, object, variable and even
expression. The property value must be enclosed in curly braces.
The values are available through this.props.PROPERTYNAME (in statefull
components) or in
the first argument of the function (in stateless).
In our case, if we talk about statefull, we get:
this.props.data - object {name: Garry, surname: Potter}
this.props.eshe_odno_svoistvo - array [1,2,3,4,5]
this.props used **only** for reading!
Let's create some news for our application.
Add an array with data to the beginning of the script tag

```
const myNews = [
{
author: 'Sasha Pechkin' ,
text: 'Thursday 4th ...'
},
{
author: 'Just Vasya' ,
text: 'I think that $ should be worth 35 rubles!'
},
{
author: 'Max Frontend' ,
text: 'It's been 2 years since previous tutorials, and $ still isn't worth 35'
},
{
author: 'Guest' ,
text: 'Free. Without SMS, about react, come in - https://maxpfrontend.ru '
```

}
];

And change the line with the News component connection as follows:

index.html

```
...
const myNews = [
{
author: 'Sasha Pechkin' ,
text: 'Thursday 4th ...'
},
{
author: 'Just Vasya' ,
text: 'I think that $ should be worth 35 rubles!'
},
{
author: 'Max Frontend' ,
text: 'It's been 2 years since previous tutorials, and $ still isn't worth 35'
},
{
author: 'Guest' ,
text: 'Free. Without SMS, about react, come in - https://maxpfrontend.ru
'
}
];
const News = () => {
return <p> Sorry, no news </p>
}
const Comments = () => {
return <p> No news - nothing to comment. </p>
}
const App = () => {
return (
<React.Fragment>
<News data = {myNews} /> {/ * added data property * /}
<Comments />
</React.Fragment>
)
}
ReactDOM.render (
<App />,
document.getElementById ('root')
);
```

...

Note that comments inside JSX are written in curly braces: {/ * text comment * /}

Please also note that JSX is not all the js code contained in the script tag,

roughly speaking JSX is HTML markup + variables / expressions. Therefore in

in other places, you can write comments in your usual way (// ... or /*...*/)

Open the react tab in the console (of course, after refreshing the page).

As a **reminder** , at this point, we have added a *data* property to our <News /> component .

It was not necessary to name the property like this, you could write, for example:

<News posledine_novosti = {my_news} />

Then in the developer console, it would look like this:

Ok, our component has a property that contains our news, but the component

cannot display them. It's easy to fix.

Let's present HTML markup for our news:


```
<div class = "news" >
<p class = "news__author" > Sasha Pechkin: </p>
<p class = "news__text" > Thursday, the fourth ... </p>
</div>
```


Question: We have markup for one item of data, we have the entire data

(array myNews). How do I display this data?

Answer: You need to create a template, go through all the variables in the array with news

and substitute values.

When you need to display a variable in a JSX markup template it is also

wrapped in curly braces. In practice, it looks easier than in theory,

so let's imagine what our JSX markup might look like:


```
this .props.data.map ( function ( item, index ) {
return (
<div key = {index} >
```

```
<p className = "news__author" > {item.author}: </p>
<p className = "news__text" > {item.text} </p>
</div>
)
})
```

1. We used the array method - *Map* . If you are unfamiliar with it, read
documentation .
2. We have wrapped the markup inside *return* in the root <div> element
. We could
wrap it in any other element, the main thing, I **remind you** - inside
return always
should return a DOM node (that is, anything wrapped in a parent
tag or in React.Fragment).
3. We used the **key** attribute (<div key = {index}>) for the parent element .
If
it is extremely simple to explain: a reactant needs uniqueness so that
all of its
the mechanisms worked correctly. By the "key" *he* will understand
with which one
the child node you are working on and which parent it belongs to.
Index - not
ideal for a key, we'll fix that next.
4. We used in the template, variable values + text, for example <p
className = "news__author"> {item.author}: </p> which could have been submitted
to
native js code as <p className = "news__author"> " + item.author + ':' </p> (empty
string + variable value + colon)
As a result of the work of the map function, we got a new array
consisting of
the react elements we need. This is the solution to our problem, we
have
just save this array in a variable, for example newsTemplate , and in
render
functions of the <News /> component return markup + "template-
variable".
We'll quickly convert News into statefull (via class ... extends):

index.html
...
const myNews = [
{

```
```

```
author: 'Sasha Pechkin' ,
text: 'Thursday 4th ...'
},
{
author: 'Just Vasya' ,
text: 'I think that S should be worth 35 rubles!'
},
{
author: 'Max Frontend' ,
text: 'It's been 2 years since previous tutorials, and S still isn't worth 35'
},
{
author: 'Guest' ,
text: 'Free. Without SMS, about react, come in - https://maxpfrontend.ru '
}
];
class News extends React . Component {
render () {
const newsTemplate = this .props.data.map ( function ( item, index ) {
return (
<div key = {index} >
<p className = "news__author" > {item.author}: </p>
<p className = "news__text" > {item.text} </p>
</div>
)
})
console .log (newsTemplate)
return (
<div className = "news" >
{newsTemplate}
</div>
)
}
}
...
```

Let's see what happened:

Not thrilled yet? The amount of code - the cat cried.

Finally, I don't want to, but I will have to destroy the magic again.

Let's get a look,

which is returned by console.log (newsTemplate) (open the Console tab).

Let's take a look at the console:

Object, object has properties ... everything is as usual in the javascript world.

Why you shouldn't use index as key

If anyone is interested in the reasons, then I will give you a comment from an old tutorial:

PS Here and throughout the course in code to display an array of news
used key index = {} . Pay attention to the following thread
comments (thanks to *DeLaVega* and *geakstr*).

The bottom line is that index is not the best option for a key, when your "items" can change
order. Our news does not change, but nevertheless, we can quickly solve our
the problem of adding a "really" unique value that will not
change if elements change index.

Of course, this property is called id;) Let's add it to the array and use as a key.

index.html

```
...
const myNews = [
{
id: 1 , // added id
author: 'Sasha Pechkin' ,
text: 'Thursday 4th ...'
},
{
id: 2 ,
author: 'Just Vasya' ,
text: 'I think that $ should be worth 35 rubles!'
},
{
id: 3 ,
author: 'Max Frontend' ,
text: 'It's been 2 years since previous tutorials, and $ still isn't worth 35'
},
{
id: 4 ,
author: 'Guest' ,
text: 'Free. Without SMS, about react, come in - https://maxpfrontend.ru
```

```
}
];
class News extends React . Component {
render () {
const newsTemplate = this .props.data.map ( function ( item ) {
return (
<div key = {item.id} > {/ * use id as key * /}
<p className = "news__author" > {item.author}: </p>
<p className = "news__text" > {item.text} </p>
</div>
)
})
return (
<div className = "news" >
{newsTemplate}
</div>
)
}
}
...
```

Total : we learned how to display the properties of a component.
Current source code . Don't forget to remove console.log.

If-else, ternary operator

Remember we had the phrase "no news"? It would be nice to display it if the news
really no.
First, let's learn how to display the total number of news, let's say at the bottom, after
news list.

36

As a participant in the "Guess the JS" game would say - I'll write it in one line. What do you think
you? Prompt:

```
class News extends React . Component {
render () {
const newsTemplate = this .props.data.map ( function ( item ) {
return (
<div key = {item.id} > {/ * use id as key * /}
<p className = "news__author" > {item.author}: </p>
<p className = "news__text" > {item.text} </p>
</div>
)
})
return (
<div className = "news" >
{newsTemplate}
{/ * this line is here * /}
</div>
)
}
}
```

Answer:

```
<strong> Total news: {this.props.data.length} </strong>
```

Play around with the *myNews* variable . Make it empty array, add / remove
elements. Refresh the page. The number of news items should work correctly.
Let's get back to our problem. The algorithm is simple:
We create the variable *newsTemplate* , if there is news - into the variable as before
we will transfer the result of the map function, otherwise we will transfer it immediately
markup that "no news".
Component News:

```
class News extends React . Component {
render () {
const {data} = this .props // similar to const data = this.props.data
```

```
let newsTemplate
if (data.length) { // if there is news, go through the map
newsTemplate = data.map ( function ( item ) {
return (
<div key = {item.id} >
<p className = "news__author" > {item.author}: </p>
<p className = "news__text" > {item.text} </p>
</div>
)
})
} else { // if there is no news, save the paragraph to a variable
newsTemplate = <p> Sorry, no news </p>
}
return (
<div className = "news" >
{newsTemplate}
<strong> Total news: {data.length} </strong>
</div>
);
}
}
```

For those who are very little familiar with js, let me remind you that:


```
if (data.length)
// can be represented as
if (data.length> 0)
```

If there is no news - why should we show that there are 0 news in total? Let's solve it with
using the css class .none , which we will add if there is no news.
Add a new style:


```
.none {
display : none;
}
```

With the .none class , everything is solved in one line again.
Change the line about the number of news as follows:

```
<strong className = {data.length> 0? ": 'none'}> Total news: {data.length}
</strong>
```

As easy as pie: *have news? 'empty class': 'class .none'*
To work with classes when there are more of them and conditions become more complicated,
you can use className (NPM package)... But now this is not necessary.
In general, the topic of working with styles in react applications is very extensive. I more
leaning towards SCSS + regular classes or styled-components.
We have hidden our strong element with a class, but with this approach, the element
stayed in the DOM tree. We can fix this by not displaying the element at all.

```
...
return (
<div className = "news" >
{newsTemplate}
{
data.length? <strong> Total news: {data.length} </strong> : null
}
</div>
);
...
```

Total : if you need to display something depending on the conditions, do it like this
the same as if react was not connected, but do not forget that the "conditions" inside the JSX
are written in curly braces. For convenience, we have used a *template variable* ,
which was announced **in advance** , and then, depending on the condition, saved in it
the necessary markup.

Source code at the moment.
PS official documentation about If-else inside JSX

Let's refactor ...

First, remove the <Comments /> component altogether (and const Comments ... respectively).
Next, let's imagine: our news has some additional
fields, the user begins to interact with them, for example "mark as read "and so on. It would be convenient for us that each news was presented as a separate component.
Objective : <News /> should render a list of <Article /> components . Each the <Article /> component should receive the appropriate data, for example: first
the instance will get the first element of the array, the second will get the second, and so on.
That is, we used to return JSX markup to map. But we can also return and component.
Try it yourself and then see the solution below.
Tip # **1** : the if-else of our <News /> component

```
if (data.length) {
newsTemplate = data.map ( function ( item ) {
return <Article key = {item.id} data = {item} />
})
} else {
newsTemplate = <p> Sorry, no news </p>
}
```

Tip # **2** (essentially a solution): <Article /> component

```
class Article extends React . Component {
render () {
const {author, text} = this .props.data
return (
<div className = "article" >
<p className = "news__author" > {author}: </p>
<p className = "news__text" > {text} </p>
</div>
)
}
}
```

Curiously, nothing else has changed.
Add the heading "News" to <App /> before the <News /> component

```
const App = () => {
return (
<React.Fragment>
<h3> News </h3>
<News data = {myNews} />
</React.Fragment>
)
}
```

Add beauties (CSS) to your liking, or take mine:

```
.none {
display : none;
}
body {
background : rgba (0, 102, 255, 0.38);
font-family : sans-serif;
}
p {
margin : 0 0 5px ;
}
.article {
background : #FFF ;
border : 1px solid rgba (0, 89, 181, 0.82);
width : 600px ;
margin : 0 0 5px ;
```

```
box-shadow : 2px 2px 5px - 1px rgb (0, 81, 202);
padding : 3px 5px ;
}
.news__author {
text-decoration : underline;
color : # 007DDC ;
}
.news__count {
margin : 10px 0 0 0 ;
display : block;
}
```

With the new styles, the script code looks like this:

index.html

```
<! DOCTYPE html>
<html>
<head>
<meta charset = "UTF-8" />
<title> React [RU] Tutorial v2 </title>
<script src = "https://unpkg.com/react@16/umd/react.development.js">
</script>
<script src = "https://unpkg.com/react-dom@16/umd/react-
dom.development.js"> </ script
>
<script src = "https://unpkg.com/babel-standalone@6.15.0/babel.min.js">
</script>
<style>
.none {
display: none;
}
body {
background: rgba (0, 102, 255, 0.38);
font-family: sans-serif;
}
p {
margin: 0 0 5px;
}
.article {
background: #FFF;
border: 1px solid rgba (0, 89, 181, 0.82);
width: 600px;
margin: 0 0 5px;
box-shadow: 2px 2px 5px -1px rgb (0, 81, 202);
padding: 3px 5px;
}
```

```css
.news__author {
text-decoration: underline;
color: # 007DDC;
}
.news__count {
margin: 10px 0 0 0;
display: block;
}
</style>
</head>
<body>
<div id = "root"> </div>
<script type = "text / babel">
const myNews = [
{
id: 1, // added id
author: 'Sasha Pechkin',
text: 'Thursday 4th ...'
},
{
id: 2,
author: 'Just Vasya',
text: 'I think that $ should be worth 35 rubles!'
},
{
id: 3,
author: 'Max Frontend',
text: 'It's been 2 years since previous tutorials, and $ still isn't worth 35'
},
{
id: 4,
author: 'Guest',
text: 'Free. Without SMS, about react, come in - https://maxpfrontend.ru '
}
];
class Article extends React.Component {
render () {
const {author, text} = this.props.data
return (
<div className = "article">
<p className = "news__author"> {author}: </p>
<p className = "news__text"> {text} </p>
</div>
)
}
}
class News extends React.Component {
render () {
const {data} = this.props
```

```
let newsTemplate
if (data.length) {
newsTemplate = data.map (function (item) {
return <Article key = {item.id} data = {item} />
})
} else {
newsTemplate = <p> Sorry, no news </p>
}
return (
<div className = "news">
{newsTemplate}
{
data.length? <strong className = {'news__count'}> Total news: {data.
length} </strong>: null
}
</div>
);
}
}
const App = () => {
return (
<React.Fragment>
<h3> News </h3>
<News data = {myNews} />
</React.Fragment>
)
}
ReactDOM.render (
<App />,
document.getElementById ('root')
);
</script>
</body>
</html>
```

In general, almost everything suits me. It remains to polish the render method a little

component <News /> . The rule is as follows: we try to keep render as possible

less code to make it easy for your colleagues to read. For this, we newsTemplate will be filled inside a new method that will be called in

render.

```
class News extends React . Component {
renderNews = () => {
const {data} = this .props
let newsTemplate = null
if (data.length) {
newsTemplate = data.map ( function ( item ) {
```

```
return <Article key = {item.id} data = {item} />
})
} else {
newsTemplate = <p> Sorry, no news </p>
}
return newsTemplate
}
render () {
const {data} = this.props
return (
<div className = "news" >
{this.renderNews ()}
{
data.length? <strong className = {'news__count'} > Total news: {data.length}
</strong> : null
}
</div>
);
}
}
```

What's remarkable about this code?
We created the renderNews method (inside the class) using the so-called "bold
arrow function "(notation methodName = () => ...). With this notation, inside
function, we do not lose this context . That is, we can refer to this.props ,
eg.
Why do n't we describe the render method through a bold arrow
function? because
that this is a method of the life cycle of a react component, and there
this "throws" itself
react.
Further, since we created renderNews as a method, it means inside the
component,
we must refer to it as this.xxx (where xxx is the name of the method, in
our
case of renderNews).
What has changed, you ask? There was a lot of code in render, now
it's a little higher The thing is
the fact that when your components grow, it is very convenient to
have a "render" well
readable, that is, one in which everything superfluous is hidden.
Let's see what happened in the end:
Source code at the moment.

Prop-types

(boring but small theoretical smoke break)

Before *proceeding* with this tutorial, remember that *PropTypes* does not work with

production version of the react. This feature is for development only, since validation is

expensive operation.

Let's break down our code:

```
const App = () => {
return (
<React.Fragment>
<h3> News </h3>
<News /> {/ * removed data transfer * /}
</React.Fragment>
)
}
```

Refresh the page - we see an error message.

Basically, everything is clear - we are trying to call the map method on *undefined* . The primitive

undefined, as you know there are no methods - an error, get your signature. Okay,

that there is not enough code and we quickly found out what the problem is. Better yet, there is

the ability to improve our position by adding *propTypes* - a special property,

which will "validate" our component.

Add another script upload to your document:

```
<script src = "https://unpkg.com/prop-types@15.6/prop-types.js"> </script>
```
Don't be confused by version 15.6 of the prop-types package. For some time now he lives his own

life, separate from react.

Make changes to the <News /> component

```
...
class News extends React.Component {
renderNews = () => {
...
}
render () {
...
}
}
```

```
// added propTypes.
// propTypes (with small letter) = News property
News.propTypes = {
data: PropTypes.array.isRequired // PropTypes (capitalized) = prop-ty library
pes
}
...
```

Refresh the page:
Much better! Based on the text of the error, we immediately understand where to dig: in render
in the App method, the data property is not specified, which is expected in News. Fairness
for sake, there is a similar message below, but the error there has a universal text.
Detailed "sheets" of the text about the error - the merit of new versions of the react. It's comfortable.
Let's restore the data property.

```
const App = () => {
return (
<React.Fragment>
<h3> News </h3>
<News data = {myNews} />
</React.Fragment>
)
}
```

Everything works again and our console is clean.

More about propTypes
I will give an excerpt from off.documentation :

```
MyComponent.propTypes = {
propTypes: {
// You can specify which primitive the property should be
optionalArray: PropTypes.array,
optionalBool: PropTypes.bool,
optionalFunc: PropTypes.func,
optionalNumber: PropTypes.number,
optionalObject: PropTypes.object,
optionalString: PropTypes.string,
optionalSymbol: PropTypes.symbol,
// ...
// You can specify that the property can be one of ...
optionalUnion: PropTypes.oneOfType ([
PropTypes.string,
PropTypes.number,
```

PropTypes.instanceOf (Message)
])
// ...
// You can specify a specific structure of the property object
optionalObjectWithShape: PropTypes.shape ({
color: PropTypes.string,
fontSize: PropTypes.number
}),
// You can specify that the property is REQUIRED
requiredFunc: React.PropTypes.func.isRequired,
// If you need to indicate that the property is simply required, and can be any primitive
wom
requiredAny: React.PropTypes.any.isRequired,
// ... (there are more options in the documentation)
}
};

According to this listing, we can translate the rule specified in the component

<News /> :

PropTypes.array.isRequired - the property must be an array and it is required must be!

I see in the eyes of some (yes, I see) that all this is some kind of useless crap.

So it is clear - there is an error, there is an opportunity to poke at it in the debugger and

look. Especially for you, the following situation: remove from the myNews array

author, for example in the third element:

```
const myNews = [
{
id: 1 ,
author: 'Sasha Pechkin' ,
text: 'Thursday 4th ...' ,
bigText: 'at four and a quarter o'clock four black dirty little imp were drawing black ink blueprint. '
},
{
id: 2 ,
author: 'Just Vasya' ,
text: 'I think $ should be worth 35 rubles!' ,
bigText: 'And the euro 42!'
},
```

```
{
id: 3 ,
// removed the author
text: 'It's been 2 years since previous tutorials, and $ still isn't worth 35' ,
bigText: 'And the euro is again above 70.'
},
{
id: 4 ,
author: 'Guest' ,
text: 'Free. Without SMS, about react, come in - https://maxpfrontend.ru ' ,
bigText: 'There is also a VK group, a telegram and a youtube channel! All infa
on the site, not p
advertising! '
}
];
```

Let's see the result:

No mistakes. But our application **doesn't work** as it should. Who's guilty? React?

The backend programmer who sent us this data?

The programmer may be to blame. But the react is definitely not. We got that in

this.props.data.author is undefined (variable is undefined). therefore

react did just that, and showed us "nothing" (in the screenshot it's just a "colon").

This error is difficult to catch.

Add *propTypes* to the <Article /> component

```
class Article extends React . Component {
render () {
...
}
}
Article.propTypes = {
data: PropTypes.shape ({
author: PropTypes.string.isRequired,
text: PropTypes.string.isRequired
})
}
```

In this case, you will receive an error message:

Isn't that wonderful?

Source code at the moment.

PS Don't forget to return the author;)

Using state

Let's get back from theory to practice: let's click on the links-buttons,
change the properties of the components ...
Oops, it won't work! Remember, properties (*this.props*) should only
be used for
reading, and for dynamic properties you need to use the so-called
"state"
(*state*).
So, meet - **this.state** ;)
Since I need to keep a minimum of theory and more practice in this
section,
let's get down to business. I propose to solve the following problem
together: *the news has*
link "more", by clicking on which - bingo, news text in full .
Let's start by changing the data:

```
const myNews = [
{
id: 1 ,
author: 'Sasha Pechkin' ,
text: 'Thursday 4th ...' ,
bigText: 'at four and a quarter o'clock four black dirty little imp were drawing
black ink blueprint. '
},
{
id: 2 ,
author: 'Just Vasya' ,
text: 'I think $ should be worth 35 rubles!' ,
bigText: 'And the euro 42!'
},
{
id: 3 ,
author: 'Max Frontend' ,
text: 'It's been 2 years since previous tutorials, and $ still isn't worth 35' ,
bigText: 'And the euro is again above 70.'
},
{
id: 4 ,
author: 'Guest' ,
```

text: 'Free. Without SMS, about react, come in - https://maxpfrontend.ru ' ,
bigText: 'There is also a VK group, a telegram and a youtube channel! All infa
on the site, not p
advertising! '
}
];

Then, we will learn how to display the full text of the news right after
the introductory text:

```
class Article extends React . Component {
render () {
const {author, text, bigText} = this .props.data // pulled bigText from date
return (
<div className = 'article' >
<p className = 'news__author' > {author}: </p>
<p className = 'news__text' > {text} </p>
<p className = 'news__big-text' > {bigText} </p>
</div>
)
}
}
Article.propTypes = {
data: PropTypes.shape ({
author: PropTypes.string.isRequired,
text: PropTypes.string.isRequired,
bigText: PropTypes.string.isRequired // added propTypes for bigText
})
}
```

Again, nothing else needs to be changed. The data will be displayed
correctly.
Let's check ...
Great, you can continue working: add a link - "more". I will give a
fragment
code:

```
...
return (
<div className = 'article' >
<p className = 'news__author' > {author}: </p>
<p className = 'news__text' > {text} </p>
<a href= "#" className='news__readmore'> More </a>
<p className = 'news__big-text' > {bigText} </p>
</div>
)
```

...

Check and if everything is ok - we are ready to work with the state of the component.

Initial state

You can work with state only in statefull components (class)
If you are defining some mutable property in a component, you need specify the initial state (in react.js terminology - *initial state*). For this, have
component, you just need to define the state property:

```
class Article extends React . Component {
state = {
visible: false , // define the initial state
}
render () {
const {author, text, bigText} = this .props.data
return (
<div className = 'article' >
<p className = 'news__author' > {author}: </p>
<p className = 'news__text' > {text} </p>
<a href= "#" className='news__readmore'> More </a>
<p className = 'news__big-text' > {bigText} </p>
</div>
)
}
}
```

Let's look in the console on the React tab:
A property has appeared *in the state* (*in state*). We will use it at the time of render.
Let's formalize the task:
if this.state.visible is === false -> draw "more", do not draw "big text";
if this.state.visible === true -> do not draw "more details", draw large text;
We will use a boolean expression inside JSX, which means curly braces, and
inside js expression.

```
class Article extends React . Component {
state = {
```

```
visible: false ,
}
render () {
const {author, text, bigText} = this .props.data
const {visible} = this .state // pulled visible from this.state
return (
<div className = 'article' >
<p className = 'news__author' > {author}: </p>
<p className = 'news__text' > {text} </p>
{/ * if not visible, then show * /
! &&'s visible <a href= "#" className='news__readmore'> More </a>
}
{/ * if visible, then show * /
visible && <p className = 'news__big-text' > {bigText} </p>
}
</div>
)
}
}
```

We used the same state variable in **two** places when describing
regular javascript expression. If you are not familiar with AND / OR,
then I recommend reading
from Cantor (Logical operators).
Please note that additional comments were not required to write
comments.
curly braces, since we were already inside the "expression" inside the
JSX.
You can check it in the browser and click on the checkbox inside the
state zone. Template already
will react. And we will continue to do all this humanly so that we can
was to click on "more".

Handling clicks - onClick

To handle the click, we need to specify the *onClick* attribute *on* the
element.
As a handler, we will have a function that changes state. For
state changes, you **must** use the **setState** method and not
overwrite the value of the variable in this.state directly.

```
class Article extends React . Component {
state = {
```

```
visible: false ,
}
handleReadMoreClck = (e) => { // added method
e.preventDefault ()
this .setState ({visible: true })
}
render () {
const {author, text, bigText} = this .props.data
const {visible} = this .state
return (
<div className = 'article' >
<p className = 'news__author' > {author}: </p>
<p className = 'news__text' > {text} </p>
{/ * added onClick * /
! visible && <a onClick = {this.handleReadMoreClck} href = "#"
className = 'news__r
eadmore ' > More </a>
}
{
visible && <p className = 'news__big-text' > {bigText} </p>
}
</div>
)
}
}
```

Check in your browser, click on the "details" link.
Each <Article /> component has its own state! Therefore, when you click on
in more detail in one of the components, only its state changes, and only this
news full text is displayed.

Total :
To save dynamic properties, the *state of the* component is used.
To handle a click, use the *onClick* property + handler function.
There are other standard events that work in the same way.
Full list here . We will review them as needed.
To change the state, the **setState** method is **used** , which takes an object with
arguments to be changed. For example, we have a state:
...

```
state = {
visible: false ,
rating: 0 ,
eshe_odno_svoistvo: 'qweqwe'
}
```
...

To change the rating, you need to write the following setState:

```
this .setState ({rating: 100500 })
```

To change all three properties:

```
this .setState ({
rating: 100500 ,
visible: true ,
eshe_odno_svoistvo: 'hello'
})
```

Also, *setState* has the ability to specify a *callback* function that will be called
after the new state is "established".

...

```
readmoreClick: function ( e ) {
e.preventDefault ();
this .setState ({visible: true }, () => {
alert ( 'The state has changed' );
});
},
```
...

Also *setState* is a possibility ... (actually there is, but we have had enough for now).
See the documentation for a complete list of setState features .
Source code at the moment.

More about state

In this section, we will see how changing *state* affects the component and a little
let's "hook" *stateless* architecture.

Changing state calls the render component

Everything is indicated in the subheading, I suggest we make sure of this:

Snippet of the `<Article />` component :

```
...
render () {
const {author, text, bigText} = this .props.data
const {visible} = this .state
console .log ( 'render' , this ); // added console.log
return (
<div className = 'article' >
<p className = 'news__author' > {author}: </p>
<p className = 'news__text' > {text} </p>
{
! visible && <a onClick = {this.handleReadMoreClck} href = "#" className =
'news__rea
dmore' > More </a>
}
{
visible && <p className = 'news__big-text' > {bigText} </p>
}
</div>
)
}
...
```

Clear your console, and click more details on any of the news:
Are you convinced? A few rules:

you cannot call *setState* inside *render:* "react is awaiting", and if changed
state - begins to redraw the component - sees what has changed
state - starts redrawing the component ...

render is an **expensive** operation, so be careful about where you are
call *setState* and what it entails. Trivial console.log can you in
help this.

Obviously, if the parent component is redrawn, then there will be
all child components are redrawn too.

In the future, we will study the different "life stages" of the
component, and make sure that
during its "redrawing" various expensive operations can be
performed and even
ajax requests. For now, just make sure that calling *setState on the*
parent will redraw
child components. To do this, I propose to create an *onClick* handler
on the phrase
"Total news".

Try it yourself.

Task : It is necessary to add to the <News /> component a state property - *counter* , in

which will store the number of clicks on the phrase "all news". I.e normal autoincrement. This property should be displayed after the number of news in

regular paragraph (<p>). It will look like this:

It is important to use this.setState ({counter: ++ this.state.counter}) in the solution , about this

we will talk in more detail after the solution, which is presented below in the form

tips and completely.

Tip # 1 : Add a state property to the <News /> component to create an initial

states.

```
...
state = {
counter: 0
}
...
```

Tip # 2 : add an *onClick* handler with a function that will increment counter (hence changing *state* , hence calling *this.setState* ...).

Solution : Complete component code <News />

```
class News extends React . Component {
state = {
counter: 0 , // added the property counter (counter)
}
handleCounter = () => { // added a new method
this .setState ({counter: ++ this .state.counter}) // in which we increment the
counter
}
renderNews = () => {
const {data} = this .props
let newsTemplate = null
if (data.length) {
newsTemplate = data.map ( function ( item ) {
return <Article key = {item.id} data = {item} />
})
} else {
newsTemplate = <p> Sorry, no news </p>
}
return newsTemplate
}
```

```
render () {
const {data} = this.props
const {counter} = this.state // pulled out counter
return (
<div className = 'news' >
{this.renderNews ()}
{/ * added onClick * /
data.length? <strong onClick = {this.handleCounter} className =
{'news__count'} >
Total news: {data.length} </strong> : null
}
<p> Total clicks: {counter} </p>
</div>
);
}
}
```

Check in your browser. If you didn't remove console.log from the
<Article /> component - by
each click on the phrase "Total news" will appear in the console 4
"redrawing".
Let's talk about: this.setState ({counter: ++ this.state.counter})
Why, it was important to use the ++ prefix notation, and not
postfix? Let's remember the theory first:
++ before the variable (prefix) - first increases it by 1, and then
returns a value;
++ after the variable (postfix) - first returns the value and then
increments
the value of the variable;
In that case, we would have to lose only 1 click, right? Check in
console like this: open React tab in console, select component
<News />, start clicking on the phrase "Total News"
Does counter change if prefix notation is used?
Yes, it changes
Does counter change if postfix notation is used?
No, it doesn't change at all. (see for yourself)
The answer lies in the official documentation:
*setState () - does not change this.state immediately, but creates a
change queue*
*states. Accessing this.state after a method call could potentially
return*
the existing (which is equivalent to the former) value.

It's time to shout - return my money back and leave ... But, not everything is so deplorable.

Now you know about this feature, and if anything you will be armed. Why so

done? Probably to optimize the library as a whole.

In general, *state* is not often used for components. With the advent flux - approach (*here*

I shed a tear and didn't rewrite in 2k18), the community became move to the side of the *stateless* approach, when *state is* not used at all (for

except for rare moments). My favorite player in this camp is **Redux** , oh

which I also wrote detailed manual in Russian (manual is not yet rewritten in a modern way, but the theory can be read).

Why are we not learning Redux now, is it worth dropping everything and reading another

tutorial? Definitely not. Continue with this course.

Situation in 2018:

There are not only Redux, but also MobX and other players. However Redux still

remains my favorite;

React for managing the state of the application as a whole, added the Context API, oh

which we will talk more about;

Pure flux is not used;

Source code with console.logs and handler for clicks on the phrase "Total news".

Working with input

First, let's clean up:

Let's remove unnecessary console.logs, remove the *handleCounter* handler and the paragraph that

displayed the number of clicks.

Then we will create a component - `<TestInput />` , which will simply render
(render) input before news list.

```
...
// --- added test input ---
class TestInput extends React . Component {
render () {
return (
<input className = 'test-input' value = 'enter value' />
)
}
}
const App = () => {
return (
<React.Fragment>
<h3> News </h3>
<TestInput /> {/ * added component output * /}
<News data = {myNews} />
</React.Fragment>
)
}
...
```

Let me remind you about the comments:
First comment added with `//` , since this comment is not
is inside JSX. And the second is found, therefore it has the form `{/ *`
comment
`* /}` . That is, JSX is not the entire code of your script, but only the parts where we mix
layout and js (usually in the return method of render).
Generally, the code doesn't work right now (but that's not because of the comment). Let's take a look at
error carefully:
You have provided a value property for a field that does not have an onChange handler.
Therefore, the rendered field is read-only. If the field is to be mutable,
use defaultValue. Either set onChange or readOnly. Check
render method of the TestInput component.
I can't help but love react for such detailed error messages.
By the way, try to change the input value now. Nothing will come of it. Here at
we have two ways, and the first one we know is to use some *state* property
as a dynamically changing input value.

Controlled components

To call *setState* , we will use the *onChange* event . Working with him is not
different from working with *onClick* or any other events. The main thing is to convey
handler function.

Take your time, let's think again:

1. We need to pass a handler function that will change some
a state variable (with *setState* , of course).
2. So we need to create the initial state (*state*).
3. If we have a component state variable, then we want
it was she who was in the *value* of our input.

Can you do it yourself? If yes - great, if not - solution below.

Tip # 1 : this is what a state + handler function might look like

```
...
state = {myValue: '' }
...
onChangeHandler = (e) => {
this .setState ({myValue: e.target.value})
},
...
```

Solution :

```
class TestInput extends React . Component {
state = {
myValue: '' ,
}
// e.currentTarget.value is used
onChangeHandler = (e) => {
this .setState ({myValue: e.currentTarget.value})
}
render () {
return (
<input
className = 'test-input'
onChange = {this.onChangeHandler}
value = {this.state.myValue}
placeholder = 'enter value' />
)
```

}
}

We have a *placeholder* - "enter value", which will be shown at the moment
loading the page, since our initial state of the input is an empty string. When
change, we set the variable *myValue* to whatever is entered in input.
Hence - input changes correctly.

e.currentTarget vs e.target

Documentation what the currentTarget property is (MDN)
Imagine a situation: you will have an onClick on a div with a text inside
in paragraph. As a result, when you click on the text in the pagraph:
e.target will be equal to paragraph (and this is true, by spec)
e.currentTarget will be equal to div (which is what we usually want)
Whoever does not understand what is at stake - you need to read
basics about event object or
whole section the basics of working with events entirely (Kantor).
Usually, we want to send input values on click ...
Task: By clicking on the button - show alert with the input text.
Try it yourself.

Hint # **1** :
You need:
add a button to <TestInput /> ;
on the button "hang" the *onClick* handler ;
in the handler function, read the value of this.state.myValue ;
Hint # **2** :
Since we need to render more than one element, we need to wrap
them in
parent element, for example in <div> </div> or React.Fragment
Solution :

```
class TestInput extends React . Component {
state = {
myValue: " ,
}
onChangeHandler = (e) => {
```

```
this .setState ({myValue: e.currentTarget.value})
}
onBtnClickHandler = (e) => {
alert ( this .state.myValue);
}
render () {
return (
<React.Fragment>
<input
className = 'test-input'
onChange = {this.onChangeHandler}
value = {this.state.myValue}
placeholder = 'enter value' />
<button onClick = {this.onBtnClickHandler}> Show alert </button>
</React.Fragment>
)
}
}
```

I suggest adding some padding for .test-input:

css / app.css

```
...
.test-input {
margin : 0 5px 5px 0 ;
}
...
```

After adding indentation in this code, nothing annoys. Or not? What do you think,
what could upset the optimization fighter here?
Answer : every time, after any change, *setState* is called for us ,
which means -
complete redrawing of the component. Not very nice. Again, a little more logic in
moment of render'a component and at the time it will get frustrated by the "responsive" input field.
We don't have any logic in the render method, so this is an unnecessary optimization for us.
However, to consider a way to create "uncontrolled components" you need to
certainly.
React documentation suggests you use in most cases

controlled components.

Uncontrolled Components (uncontrolled component)

The main difference uncontrolled component from the controlled one in that it has
there is no change handler, which means there are no constant
setState calls and redrawings.
In order to read the value of an uncontrolled component, use
refs mechanism.
For an uncontrolled component at boot time, you can specify
defaultValue .
Let's start in order:

1. Remove the handler *onChange*
2. Remove *state*
3. *Specify defaultValue* = empty string (defaultValue = '') instead of *value*
4. In the constructor method of the component (op-pa), specify this.input
= React.createRef ();
5. Add an attribute *ref to the* input equal to this.input (which was created
in the constructor)

```
class TestInput extends React . Component {
constructor (props) {
super (props)
this .input = React.createRef ()
}
onBtnClickHandler = (e) => { // this entry is not working now
alert ( this .state.myValue);
}
render () {
return (
<React.Fragment>
<input
className = 'test-input'
defaultValue = ''
placeholder = 'enter value'
```

```
ref = {this.input}
/>
<button onClick = {this.onBtnClickHandler}> Show alert </button>
</React.Fragment>
)
}
}
```

Refresh the page, try entering a value. Working? Working!
Now we need to learn how to read the value: *rewrite*
onBtnClickHandler
in the following way:

```
onBtnClickHandler = () => {
alert ( this .input.current.value)
},
```

AT documentation there is also an example of using refs and file
access,
loaded via <input type = "file" /> .
During this lesson, we learned with you not to call expensive *setState*
and *render* on "each
sneeze ".
PS Of course, in this case, there is no performance gain. Both
approaches will work well.
Option with controlled and uncontrolled components, work with
defaultValue and *state* are the same for all form elements.

I highly recommend looking at the documentation page in English by
elements
forms
Source code at the moment (including *alert* and *console.log*). So far
left *input*
with *ref* .

Component life cycle

Favorite phrase in this tutorial "let's imagine a problem":
We have rendered a component that has an input, and we want the focus immediately
settled into it. When I first thought "how to do it", I didn't even think of
what to answer.
Okay, let's say I know that I can reach the DOM element through *this.input.current* and call the native focus () method , but at what point to knock?
What kind of "moments" are there?

Lifecycle methods

Each component has a *lifecycle* : the component will be mounted, the component has been rendered, the component will be removed, and so on ...
All these phases have methods, the so-called *lifecycle-methods* . Full list as
always in the documentation. I suggest you watch it again at the end of the lesson, but for now
enough information here.
A little remark: here I will list some of the most popular methods, and there will be old methods too, as many have not yet cleansed them out. Old methods
will be marked with a [DEPRECATED] tag
Let's start:
componentWillMount - the component will be mounted. At the moment we do not have
the ability to view DOM elements. **[DEPRECATED]**
componentDidMount - the component is mounted. At the moment we have
the ability to use *refs* , and therefore this is the very place where we would like to indicate the focus setting. Also, timeouts, ajax requests and
interfacing with other libraries is worth handling **here** .
This method is suitable for solving our problem:

```
class TestInput extends React . Component {
constructor (props) {
super (props)
```

```
this .input = React.createRef ()
}
componentDidMount () {
// set focus to input
this .input.current.focus ()
}
onBtnClickHandler = () => {
alert ( this .input.current.value)
}
render () {
return (
<React.Fragment>
<input
className = 'test-input'
defaultValue = "
placeholder = 'enter value'
ref = {this.input}
/>
<button onClick = {this.onBtnClickHandler}> Show alert </button>
</React.Fragment>
)
}
}
```

The principle is the same: we find the DOM node, read its property /
call it
native method, in this case, we call the method focus () . Accessing
the DOM
elements directly is a **very rare practice** in React.
componentWillReceiveProps - the component receives new *props* .
This method is not
called at the time of the first render. The official documentation is
very
a good example, perhaps I'll copy it: **[DEPRECATED]**


```
componentWillReceiveProps (nextProps) {
this .setState ({
likesIncreasing: nextProps.likeCount> this .props.likeCount
});
}
```

Note: at this point, the old *props* are available as *this.props* , and the
new ones
props are available as **nextProps** function arguments.
Likewise, if you call *setState* inside this method, **it will not be** called.
additional *render* .

shouldComponentUpdate - Should the component update? Actually, usually the reactant understands well itself. But sometimes manual control allows

significantly speed up work in "bottlenecks". You need to work with this method

very neat.

componentWillUpdate - Called right before *render* when new *props* and *state*

received. *SetState* cannot be called in this method .

[DEPRECATED]

componentDidUpdate - Called immediately after *render* . Not called at the moment

the first render of the component.

componentWillUnmount - called before the component is removed from

DOM.

Of course, the documentation describes everything in much more detail. I recommend with her

familiarize.

Here **I want to draw your attention to the** fact that most often in old code or old

the tutorials will come across the componentWillReceiveProps method , which Facebook-

the team suggests replacing with getDerivedStateFromProps .

Total : the main point of this lesson: a component has stages of life, "in which

you can write code. "Yes, let me act here as a" bad programmer "who advises you to write your bikes at different stages in the life of a component, but

this is how you get up to speed quickly. Put *console.log* and see when it is

works. Think about how you can use it for your own purposes.

If you belong to the "right" type of programmer - please, that's all lifecycle methods . Learn, re-read, realize - and write code without bugs;)

Total : there are several lifecycle methods, thanks to which we are almost

stopped "climbing" in the DOM, and if we do it, then it is consciously.

Source code at the moment.

Working with a form

In this tutorial, we will turn our *input* into a form for adding news. Let's learn
work with checkboxes, the disabled attribute of the button and other standard for such
tasks with things.
The result of adding news, for now, again, will be *alert* with the text of the news.
Rename <TestInput /> to <Add /> and render the following form in it: author
(*input*), news text (*textarea*), "I agree with the rules" (*checkbox*),
"show alert"
(*button*).
Along the way, we will change the names of the classes, remove autofocus, remove unnecessary handlers and
move the <Add /> component in front of the "News" heading.
In total, the template for "adding news" will look like this:

```
class Add extends React . Component {
onBtnClickHandler = (e) => {
e.preventDefault ()
}
render () {
return (
<form className = 'add'>
<input
type = 'text'
className = 'add__author'
placeholder = 'Your name'
/>
<textarea
className = 'add__text'
placeholder = 'News text'
> </textarea>
<label className = 'add__checkrule'>
```

```
<input type = 'checkbox' /> I agree with the rules
</label>
<button
className = 'add__btn'
onClick = {this.onBtnClickHandler}>
Show alert
</button>
</form>
)
}
}
```

If you don't mind my styling, you can take the styles for the <Add /> component :

```
.add {
margin : 0 5px 5px 0 ;
width : 210px ;
border : 1px dashed rgba (0, 89, 181, 0.82);
padding : 5px ;
}
.add__author, .add__text, .add__btn, .add__checkrule {
display : block;
margin : 0 0 5px 0 ;
padding : 5px ;
width : 94% ;
border : 1px solid rgba (0, 89, 181, 0.82);
}
.add__checkrule {
border : none;
font-size : 12px ;
}
.add__btn {
box-sizing : content-box;
color : #FFF ;
text-transform : uppercase;
background : # 007DDC ;
}
.add__btn: disabled {
background : #CCC ;
color : # 999 ;
}
```

Since we are close to the final, I would like to load you with work.
Task : now the input "your name" and the text area are just "blank".
Need to make them
controlled.

70

Hint :

create state (initial state)
add handlers to change the name and text of the news
in the value of the elements write the value of the variable from the
state
Solution : (the code is not perfect now, but understandable. We will
refactor at the end
section)


```
class Add extends React . Component {
state = { // added the initial state
name: " ,
text: " ,
}
onBtnClickHandler = (e) => {
e.preventDefault ()
}
handleNameChange = (e) => {handler in which we update name
this .setState ({name: e.currentTarget.value})
}
handleTextChange = (e) => {handler in which we update text
this .setState ({text: e.currentTarget.value})
}
render () {
const {name, text} = this .state // pulled values from the state
// added value for name and for textarea
return (
<form className = 'add'>
<input
type = 'text'
onChange = {this.handleNameChange}
className = 'add__author'
placeholder = 'Your name'
value = {name}
/>
<textarea
onChange = {this.handleTextChange}
className = 'add__text'
placeholder = 'News text'
value = {text}
> </textarea>
<label className = 'add__checkrule'>
<input type = 'checkbox' /> I agree with the rules
</label>
<button
className = 'add__btn'
onClick = {this.onBtnClickHandler}>
Show alert
```

```
</button>
</form>
)
}
}
```

The inputs started working and we have a very nice bonus: name and news text
stored in this.state. Conveniently? Of course. Imagine what we will do
form validation. We will have **actual values** at any time
name and text news! Still not happy? A little patience and we'll get to validation ...
However, first, let's make the checkbox + button for sending news work.
Let's turn off the "show alert" button if the checkbox is not checked. There are 2
options - use *state* or not. For our task, no
there will be no performance problems if we use *state* . Climb in
DOM (even with refs) in React apps is not the best option.
Let's break down the task into stages, it is necessary:
add value to state for checkbox (true / false);
add the *disabled* attribute to the button equal to the value from the
state ;
add a handler function;
Try it yourself or see the solution:

```
class Add extends React . Component {
state = {
name: " ,
text: " ,
agree: false , // new state value - agree (boolean)
}
onBtnClickHandler = (e) => {
e.preventDefault ()
}
handleNameChange = (e) => {
this .setState ({name: e.currentTarget.value})
}
handleTextChange = (e) => {
this .setState ({text: e.currentTarget.value})
}
handleCheckboxChange = (e) => { // handler for clicks on the checkbox
// read the checked property to set true / false
this .setState ({agree: e.currentTarget.checked})
}
```

```
render () {
const {name, text, agree} = this .state
return (
<form className = 'add'>
<input
type = 'text'
onChange = {this.handleNameChange}
className = 'add__author'
placeholder = 'Your name'
value = {name}
/>
<textarea
onChange = {this.handleTextChange}
className = 'add__text'
placeholder = 'News text'
value = {text}
> </textarea>
<label className = 'add__checkrule'>
<input type = 'checkbox' onChange = {this.handleCheckboxChange} /> I agree with
rules
</label>
{/ * button added disabled equal to (NOT agree) * /}
<button
className = 'add__btn'
onClick = {this.onBtnClickHandler}
disabled = {! agree}>
Show alert
</button>
</form>
)
}
}
```

Since the state is changed by clicking in the checkbox, redrawing is called
(the render method will work). This means that we will always have the current agree value in
disabled attribute.
I have nothing more to comment here for those who know JavaScript basics. For those,
who doesn't know:
checked (Cantor);
Change: change, input, cut, copy, paste (Cantor)
disabled = true will mean the button is disabled. The button should be disabled when agree = false (that is, the checkbox is not checked), then we
do negation (NOT) with an exclamation mark;

To add news, we just need to generate a code that will display in *alert* name and text of news. I think this task is definitely within your power.

Solution :

```
...
onBtnClickHandler = (e) => {
e.preventDefault ()
const {name, text} = this .state
alert (name + '\ n' + text) // \ n = line break
}
```

Lock the button if not all fields are filled

The promised validation has arrived. More precisely, " *Validation Part 1: The Beginning* ".
Why Part 1? Because, form validation and generally working with a form is one of the
the most meticulous tasks. You need to show clear error messages, highlight an incorrectly filled field, block the submit button, validate fields according to certain rules and so on.
At the moment, we will add to the condition (that the checkbox is checked) only one simple
condition: the name and text fields must be filled. And not spaces.
How would such a problem be solved without react? We would probably have a *validate* function ,
which would be called for every change in the fields being checked. It would be necessary
generate and listen to event ...
I think you take the hint. You can't do without *state* here , and this is exactly the place where
it is more convenient to use the **state** , rather than refs.
Try it yourself and then check the solution.
Task : if nothing (or spaces) is entered in the "name" or "text" field - the button
"show alert" should be grayed out.

Tip # **1** : Use the standard trim () method to remove whitespace
Tip # **2** : you need to pass the result of work in the *disabled* attribute
the *validate* function (which needs to be created as a component method so that
access to *this.state*). Example:

```
validate = () => {
// some conditions
// returns true or false
}
...
<button disabled = { this .validate ()} ...>
...
```

Solution :

```
class Add extends React . Component {
state = {
name: " ,
text: " ,
agree: false ,
}
...
validate = () => {
const {name, text, agree} = this .state
if (name.trim () && text.trim () && agree) {
return true
}
return false
}
render () {
const {name, text, agree} = this .state
return (
<form className = 'add' >
...
<button
className = 'add__btn'
onClick = {this.onBtnClickHandler}
disabled = {! this.validate ()} >
Show alert
</button>
</form>
)
}
}
```

How is it? Not much fun? If yes, then you have problems with JavaScript basics and
you need to pull them up. And if, on the whole, it's order - I congratulate you, we are almost
goals.

Let's refactor copy-paste

There is a problem:

```
handleNameChange = (e) => {
this .setState ({name: e.currentTarget.value})
}
handleTextChange = (e) => {
this .setState ({text: e.currentTarget.value})
}
```

Very similar methods. Can they be unified? Sure.
you need to add a computed key value;
understand where we will read the key from;
The key will be read from the element id. The idea is this: write the same string to id,
as the value of the key in state, that is, for name - we will give the input id = 'name' , and for
textarea - id = 'text'

Ready?

```
class Add extends React . Component {
...
handleChange = (e) => {
const {id, value} = e.currentTarget
this .setState ({[id]: e.currentTarget.value})
}
...
render () {
const {name, text, agree} = this .state
return (
<form className = 'add' >
<input
id = 'name'
type = 'text'
onChange = {this.handleChange}
className = 'add__author'
placeholder = 'Your name'
value = {name}
/>
<textarea
id = 'text'
onChange = {this.handleChange}
className = 'add__text'
placeholder = 'News text'
value = {text}
> </textarea>
...
</form>
)
}
}
```

From e.currentTarget we can read id and value . Next, we write to the state by the required key is the value.

The computed key value is one of the most painful topics for newbies.

We carefully read (and re-read) the lesson from Cantor's textbook: Objects as

associative arrays

Total : we learned how to work with the form. Launched pre-server validation.

Understood and realized that knowledge of the basics of JavaScript is an incredible "boost" in learning

React. Yes, without the basics, you can read tutorials and complete tasks, but believe me, if

if you pick up the basics first, React will become your friend much faster.

Source code at the moment.

Add news

What is news posting?

1. This is the form in which we enter the required data.

2. This is the "news feed" that displays our data.

This problem has a lot of solutions. We'll start with the canonical option: in the common parent (<App />) we will store the state with news. Into component

<Add /> we will pass a function (since in props we can pass that whatever), which will have access to the state with the news and which in turn

will add news to this state.

Since the state of <App /> will change, all children (including the news feed

<News />) will be redrawn, and therefore we will see the added news.

Interaction from child to parent

Step 1 : create a news state in <App /> (and therefore rewrite App from stateless to statefull):

```
class App extends React . Component {
```

```
state = {
news: myNews, // we put the value from the variable into the initial state
}
render () {
return (
<React.Fragment>
<Add />
<h3> News </h3>
{/ * read news from this.state * /}
<News data = {this.state.news} />
</React.Fragment>
)
}
}
```

Remarkably, we have changed the data source for <News /> , but the component
works as if nothing had happened. Conveniently!

Step 2: pass a handler function to Add

```
class App extends React . Component {
state = {
news: myNews,
}
handleAddNews = () => {
console .log ( 'I was called from Add, but I have access to this.state from App!' , this
.state)
}
render () {
return (
<React.Fragment>
<Add onAddNews = {this.handleAddNews} />
<h3> News </h3>
<News data = {this.state.news} />
</React.Fragment>
)
}
}
```

Step 3: call the function from <Add /> , don't forget about *PropTypes* .

```
class Add extends React . Component {
state = {
name: " ,
text: " ,
agree: false ,
}
onBtnClickHandler = (e) => {
e.preventDefault ()
const {name, text} = this .state
```

78

```
// alert (name + '\ n' + text)
// call alert instead
this .props.onAddNews ()
}

...
render () {
const {name, text, agree} = this .state
return (
<form className = 'add' >

...
<button
className = 'add__ btn'
onClick = {this.onBtnClickHandler}
disabled = {! this.validate ()} >
Show alert
</button>
</form>
)
}
}
Add.propTypes = {
onAddNews: PropTypes.func.isRequired, // func is used to check if fun is passed
ction
}
```

Let's check:

Step 4: from <Add /> we will transfer an object with news.

```
class Add extends React . Component {

...
onBtnClickHandler = (e) => {
e.preventDefault ()
const {name, text} = this .state
// pass name and text
// we don't have big text :(
this .props.onAddNews ({name, text})
}

...
}
```

Step 5: we will write the resulting object to the first place in the array with news
in <App /> . Of course, we will update the array via *setState* .

```
class App extends React . Component {

...
handleAddNews = (data) => {
// first we form an array based on
// everything that was already in the news
// and put it all in a new array +
// put new news at the beginning of the array
const nextNews = [data, ... this.state.news]
// then update the new news array in this.state.news
```

```
this .setState ({news: nextNews})
}
...
}
```

Let's check?
Okay, this is a great case (real work case).

First : we were almost diligent learners and made propTypes for `<Article`
`/>` . It is immediately clear from the error: we do not pass the *author* value (because we
passing in *name*).
Second : we messed up, and forgot to add propTypes for `<Article />`
id property. It's good that there is not enough code and the error was immediately found. Don't forget about
listing all properties in `propTypes` is a super cheat sheet.
Third : we do not pass `id` and `bigText` from `<Add />` .
However, it should be noted that we have added speakers to our application!
The news is added, and the news counter works (and we don't touched). Who is already celebrating - well done, but who wants to fix all the mistakes and pass
work for five - welcome to the final point of the main course.

Work on bugs

I would like you to fix all this yourself. But in order not to be an author who
"oops, jamb, let me give it to you for homework", I will do everything and describe. Just
try it. You can do it. Practice decides. Be sure to always practice for fixing the material.
Task :

add textarea for bigText to add form;
pass author;
pass id (can be done via timestamp (timestamp in ms): `+ new`
`Date ()`). For a teaching example, this will suffice;

fix propTypes in `<News />`

Solution :

The complete code for what is in `<body />` (with comments on the latest changes)

```
<body>
<div id = "root" > </div>
<script type = "text / babel" >
const myNews = [
{
id: 1 ,
author: 'Sasha Pechkin' ,
text: 'Thursday 4th ...' ,
bigText: 'at four and a quarter o'clock four black dirty little devil
they drew a drawing in black ink. '
},
{
id: 2 ,
author: 'Just Vasya' ,
text: 'I think that $ should be worth 35 rubles!' ,
bigText: 'And the euro 42!'
},
{
id: 3 ,
author: 'Max Frontend' ,
text: 'It's been 2 years since previous tutorials, and $ still isn't worth 35' ,
bigText: 'And the euro is again above 70.'
},
{
id: 4 ,
author: 'Guest' ,
text: 'Free. Without SMS, about react, come in - https://maxpfrontend.ru ' ,
bigText: 'There is also a VK group, a telegram and a youtube channel! All infa on the
site,
not advertising! '
}
];
class Article extends React . Component {
state = {
visible: false ,
}
handleReadMoreClck = (e) => {
e.preventDefault ()
this .setState ({visible: true })
}
render () {
const {author, text, bigText} = this .props.data
const {visible} = this .state
return (
```

```
<div className = 'article' >
<p className = 'news__author' > {author}: </p>
<p className = 'news__text' > {text} </p>
{
! visible && <a onClick = {this.handleReadMoreClck} href = "#" className = 'new
s__readmore ' > More </a>
}
{
visible && <p className = 'news__ big-text' > {bigText} </p>
}
</div>
)
}
}
Article.propTypes = {
data: PropTypes.shape ({
id: PropTypes.number.isRequired, // added id, this number, required
author: PropTypes.string.isRequired,
text: PropTypes.string.isRequired,
bigText: PropTypes.string.isRequired
})
}
class News extends React . Component {
// removed the old state counter: 0 (old unnecessary code)
renderNews = () => {
const {data} = this .props
let newsTemplate = null
if (data.length) {
newsTemplate = data.map ( function ( item ) {
return <Article key = {item.id} data = {item} />
})
} else {
newsTemplate = <p> Sorry, no news </p>
}
return newsTemplate
}
render () {
const {data} = this.props
return (
<div className = 'news'>
{this.renderNews ()}
{
data.length? <strong className = {'news__count'}> Total news: {data.le
ngth} </strong>: null
}
</div>
);
}
}
News.propTypes = {
data: PropTypes.array.isRequired
}
class Add extends React.Component {
state = {
```

```
name: ",
text: ",
bigText: ", // added bigText
agree: false,
}
onBtnClickHandler = (e) => {
e.preventDefault ()
const {name, text, bigText} = this.state // pulled out the same way bigText
this.props.onAddNews ({
id: + new Date (), // id stores the number of milliseconds since 1 Jan
Varya 1970 in UTC time zone
author: name, // save name in the author field
text,
bigText,
})
}
handleChange = (e) => {
const {id, value} = e.currentTarget
this.setState ({[id]: e.currentTarget.value})
}
handleCheckboxChange = (e) => {
this.setState ({agree: e.currentTarget.checked})
}
validate = () => {
const {name, text, agree} = this.state
if (name.trim () && text.trim () && agree) {
return true
}
return false
}
render () {
const {name, text, bigText, agree} = this.state
return (
<form className = 'add'>
<input
id = 'name'
type = 'text'
onChange = {this.handleChange}
className = 'add__author'
placeholder = 'Your name'
value = {name}
/>
<textarea
id = 'text'
onChange = {this.handleChange}
className = 'add__text'
placeholder = 'News text'
value = {text}
> </textarea>
{/ * added bigText * /}
<textarea
id = 'bigText'
onChange = {this.handleChange}
className = 'add__text'
```

```
placeholder = 'News text in detail'
value = {bigText}
> </textarea>
<label className = 'add__checkrule'>
<input type = 'checkbox' onChange = {this.handleCheckboxChange} /> I agree
n with rules
</label>
<button
className = 'add__btn'
onClick = {this.onBtnClickHandler}
disabled = {! this.validate ()}>
Show alert
</button>
</form>
)
}
}
Add.propTypes = {
onAddNews: PropTypes.func.isRequired,
}
class App extends React.Component {
state = {
news: myNews,
}
handleAddNews = (data) => {
const nextNews = [data, ... this.state.news]
this.setState ({news: nextNews})
}
render () {
return (
<React.Fragment>
<Add onAddNews = {this.handleAddNews} />
<h3> News </h3>
<News data = {this.state.news} />
</React.Fragment>
)
}
}
ReactDOM.render (
<App />,
document.getElementById ('root')
);
</script>
</body>
```

Done!
Source code at the moment.

Outcome

What have you learned so far:

Create components (using function and using class);

However, what is the difference besides the abbreviated and detailed notation? [1]

Pass properties (props) and read them;

Communicate from the child with the parent (via the function passed to props);

Make forks in templates (if / else, &&, etc.)

Work with mutable component state (state)

Work with the form (controlled and uncontrolled components)

Acquainted with life cycle methods

Actually only with componentDidMount and render [2]

[1] - the difference is that the stateless component has a built-in "light" check in

shouldComponentUpdate . She is invisible, but she is. This item can be attributed to the topic

optimizing redrawing of your components.

[2] - this point is covered in the second series (about Redux), but since the Redux tutorial is not yet

rewritten, I think it is worth "pumping" the example with the news here and now.

Also, there is an inconvenience that you have heard about create-react-app imports and so on, and

there is none of this in the manual here. Of course, this is done so that the management

was as dry as possible and on the topic. However, I would like to add this to

updated version.

Therefore, I do not say goodbye to you and invite you to taste the basics in additional chapters,

in which I will be extremely brief so as not to inflate the volume.

I remind you that a lot of free and not so much materials come out in my

"social spaces":

Schedule of streams and webinars (the site has text versions of webinars)

Youtube channel with recordings of webinars and streams

Group vkontakte

Channel in telegram

Twitter

Create-react-app

Here I will be very brief: facebook rolled out a convenient tool for starting
applications . New syntax, imports, testing, reloading supported
change pages, linter and much more.
We will not understand all the diversity now. Purpose: to split index.html into
components, connect them, put them in order.
Copy index.html somewhere for memory, we will split it into small ones soon
convenient components.
Installing and running create-react-app

```
npx create-react-app my-app
cd my-app
npm start
```

If you are not familiar with these commands, then you need to install yourself node.js and
enter them in the terminal after.
After launching, we will get the following picture in the browser:

And the following file structure:

```
+ - node_modules (packages for the application are located here)
+ - public (public files such as index.html and favicon are located here)
+ - src (the App component already lives here)
+ - .gitignore (file for git)
+ - package.json (file with project dependencies)
+ - README.md (project description)
+ - yarn.lock (it may or may not be - also refers to the topic of dependencies
kta)
```

Let's restore the balance in src

src / App.css (copy all our styles)

```css
.none {
display : none;
}
body {
background : rgba (0, 102, 255, 0.38);
font-family : sans-serif;
}
p {
margin : 0 0 5px ;
```

```css
}
.article {
background : #FFF ;
border : 1px solid rgba (0, 89, 181, 0.82);
width : 600px ;
margin : 0 0 5px ;
box-shadow : 2px 2px 5px - 1px rgb (0, 81, 202);
padding : 3px 5px ;
}
.news__author {
text-decoration : underline;
color : # 007DDC ;
}
.news__count {
margin : 10px 0 0 ;
display : block;
}
.test-input {
margin : 0 5px 5px 0 ;
}
.add {
margin : 0 5px 5px 0 ;
width : 210px ;
border : 1px dashed rgba (0, 89, 181, 0.82);
padding : 5px ;
}
.add__author, .add__text, .add__btn, .add__checkrule {
display : block;
margin : 0 0 5px 0 ;
padding : 5px ;
width : 94% ;
border : 1px solid rgba (0, 89, 181, 0.82);
}
.add__checkrule {
border : none;
font-size : 12px ;
}
.add__btn {
box-sizing : content-box;
color : #FFF ;
text-transform : uppercase;
background : # 007DDC ;
}
.add__btn: disabled {
background : #CCC ;
color : # 999 ;
}
```

src / App.js (copy almost everything from the script tag)

```jsx
import React from 'react' ; // connect the React library
import './App.css' ; // connect the stylesheet
```

```jsx
// further copied from the script tag
const myNews = [
{
id: 1 ,
author: "Sasha Pechkin" ,
text: "Thursday, the fourth ..." ,
bigText:
"at four and a quarter o'clock, four black grimy little imp were drawing black
and ink drawing. "
},
{
id: 2 ,
author: "Just Vasya" ,
text: "I think that $ should be worth 35 rubles!" ,
bigText: "And the euro 42!"
},
{
id: 3 ,
author: "Max Frontend" ,
text: "It's been 2 years since previous tutorials, and $ 35 still isn't worth $ 35" ,
bigText: "And the euro is again above 70."
},
{
id: 4 ,
author: "Guest" ,
text: "Free. Without SMS, about react, come in - https://maxpfrontend.ru" ,
bigText:
"There is also a VK group, a telegram and a youtube channel! All infa on the site, not
advertising!"
}
];
class Article extends React . Component {
state = {
visible: false
};
handleReadMoreClck = e => {
e.preventDefault ();
this .setState ({visible: true });
};
render () {
const {author, text, bigText} = this .props.data;
const {visible} = this .state;
return (
<div className = "article" >
<p className = "news__author" > {author}: </p>
<p className = "news__text" > {text} </p>
{! visible && (
<a
onClick = {this.handleReadMoreClck}
href = "#"
className = "news__readmore"
>
More details
</a>
```

```
)}
{visible && <p className = "news__big-text" > {bigText} </p> }
</div>
);
}
}
Article.propTypes = {
data: PropTypes.shape ({
id: PropTypes.number.isRequired, // added id, this number, required
author: PropTypes.string.isRequired,
text: PropTypes.string.isRequired,
bigText: PropTypes.string.isRequired
})
};
class News extends React . Component {
renderNews = () => {
const {data} = this .props;
let newsTemplate = null ;
if (data.length) {
newsTemplate = data.map ( function ( item ) {
return <Article key = {item.id} data = {item} />;
});
} else {
newsTemplate = <p> Sorry, no news </p>;
}
return newsTemplate;
};
render () {
const {data} = this.props;
return (
<div className = "news">
{this.renderNews ()}
{data.length? (
<strong className = {"news__count"}>
Total news: {data.length}
</strong>
): null}
</div>
);
}
}
News.propTypes = {
data: PropTypes.array.isRequired
};
class Add extends React.Component {
state = {
name: "",
text: "",
bigText: "",
agree: false
};
onBtnClickHandler = e => {
e.preventDefault ();
const {name, text, bigText} = this.state;
```

```
this.props.onAddNews ({
id: + new Date (),
author: name,
text,
bigText
});
};
handleChange = e => {
const {id, value} = e.currentTarget;
this.setState ({[id]: e.currentTarget.value});
};
handleCheckboxChange = e => {
this.setState ({agree: e.currentTarget.checked});
};
validate = () => {
const {name, text, agree} = this.state;
if (name.trim () && text.trim () && agree) {
return true;
}
return false;
};
render () {
const {name, text, bigText, agree} = this.state;
return (
<form className = "add">
<input
id = "name"
type = "text"
onChange = {this.handleChange}
className = "add__author"
placeholder = "Your name"
value = {name}
/>
<textarea
id = "text"
onChange = {this.handleChange}
className = "add__text"
placeholder = "News text"
value = {text}
/>
<textarea
id = "bigText"
onChange = {this.handleChange}
className = "add__text"
placeholder = "News text in detail"
value = {bigText}
/>
<label className = "add__checkrule">
<input type = "checkbox" onChange = {this.handleCheckboxChange} /> I
agree with the rules
</label>
<button
className = "add__btn"
onClick = {this.onBtnClickHandler}
```

```
disabled = {! this.validate ()}
>
Show alert
</button>
</form>
);
}
}
Add.propTypes = {
onAddNews: PropTypes.func.isRequired
};
class App extends React.Component {
state = {
news: myNews
};
handleAddNews = data => {
const nextNews = [data, ... this.state.news];
this.setState ({news: nextNews});
};
render () {
return (
<React.Fragment>
<Add onAddNews = {this.handleAddNews} />
<h3> News </h3>
<News data = {this.state.news} />
</React.Fragment>
);
}
}
// copied everything except ReactDOM.render
// added export
export default App;
```

Delete the src / Logo.svg file, don't touch the rest, but you can look :)
Create-react-app (CRA) on every change in files inside src directory -
reloads the page in the browser.
We don't have PropTypes in the project. Since it used to be a script
tag, now we need
npm package.
Stop create-react-app in terminal and add package prop-types

```
npm install --save prop-types
```

I do not give examples for yarn here, because if you have yarn you
are already aware of how
put packages through it.
Include PropTypes at the beginning of the file:
src / App.js

```
import React from 'react'
import PropTypes from 'prop-types'
```

```
import './App.css'
...
```

Run the application again:

```
npm start
```

Total : we have transferred the application to CRA.

Source code at the moment (added prettier config - .prettierrc, not pay attention).

Tidy

Run the application if you don't have it running (npm start).

As you remember in the last screenshot, we had warnings from eslint . eslint -

helper tool that helps keep your code clean, by

at the moment we have the following problems:

```
./src/App.js
Line 50: Links must not point to "#". Use a more descriptive href or use a button
instead jsx-a11y / href-no-hash
Line 126: 'value' is assigned a value but never used
no-unused-vars
Line 140: 'agree' is assigned a value but never used
no-unused-vars
```

Line 50: the link should have an href attribute not #, but something more intelligible

(replace with '#readmore').

Line 126 - value - not used, correct:

```
// it was
const {id, value} = e.currentTarget
this .setState ({[id]: e.currentTarget.value})
// became
const {id, value} = e.currentTarget
this .setState ({[id]: value})
```

Line 140 - agree - not used, correct:

```
// It was
const {name, text, bigText, agree} = this .state
// became
const {name, text, bigText} = this .state
```

Maintain your code without warning. If you don't know what this is about,

for example, the rule worked no-unused-vars , don't be lazy. Explore the documentation on

eslint.org

Imports

Our task is to split the huge src / App.js file into components.
The following imports are supported:
import A from 'A' // import by default
import {B} from 'B' // named import
import * as C from 'C' // import "everything" into namespace C
On the other hand, the following exports are supported:
export default A // export by default
export const B // named export
We will create several files, in each of which we will use
named exports. Then we import into App.
Create a src / components directory and in it create files for each
component other than <App />.
Let's see how to create a file using the <Article /> example :
src / components / Article.js

```
import React from 'react' // we must import the required packages in each file
import PropTypes from 'prop-types' // Article has react and prop-types
// then just copied everything except the last line
class Article extends React . Component {
state = {
visible: false ,
}
handleReadMoreClck = e => {
e.preventDefault ()
this .setState ({visible: true })
}
render () {
const {author, text, bigText} = this .props.data
const {visible} = this .state
return (
<div className = "article" >
<p className = "news__author" > {author}: </p>
<p className = "news__text" > {text} </p>
{! visible && (
<a
onClick = {this.handleReadMoreClck}
href = "#readmore"
className = "news__readmore"
>
More details
</a>
)}
{visible && <p className = "news__big-text" > {bigText} </p> }
</div>
)
}
}
Article.propTypes = {
data: PropTypes.shape ({
id: PropTypes.number.isRequired, // added id. this number, required
author: PropTypes.string.isRequired,
text: PropTypes.string.isRequired,
bigText: PropTypes.string.isRequired,
}),
}
```

export {Article} // named export

Arrange the rest of the files in the same way.
You should get the following structure:
In this case, you need to add imports to *App.js* and *News.js*

src / App.js

```
import React from 'react'
// import of the prop-types package has been removed, as this file does not use prop-types
import {Add} from './components/Add' // . = current directory,
import {News} from './components/News' // then we go to the components directory and to
required component
import './App.css'
const myNews = [
{
id: 1 ,
author: 'Sasha Pechkin' ,
...
```

src / components / News.js

```
import React from 'react'
import PropTypes from 'prop-types'
import {Article} from './Article' // no need to go to components, since we are already at this
oh directory
class News extends React . Component {
renderNews = () => {
...
```

I think the principle is clear: in each file we import what we need regarding this file.
to go up one level - '../'
to two levels higher - '../../'
to start searching in the current directory - './'
to find the Name component in the current directory in components - './components/Name'
to import from library - 'library name'
Our *App.js* has *become* noticeably thinner. It has become more convenient to navigate through the code.
myNews can also be thrown out of this file.
src / data / newsData.json (export json structure by default)

```
[
{
"id" : 1 ,
"author" : "Sasha Pechkin" ,
"text" : "On Thursday, the fourth ..." ,
"bigText" :
"at four and a quarter o'clock, four black grimy little imp were drawing black
and ink drawing. "
},
{
"id" : 2 ,
```

"author" : "Just Vasya" ,
"text" : "I think that $ should be worth 35 rubles!" ,
"bigText" : "And the euro 42!"
},
{
"id" : 3 ,
"author" : "Max Frontend" ,
"text" : "2 years have passed since the last textbooks, and the $ 35 is still not worth" ,
"bigText" : "And the euro is again above 70."
},
{
"id" : 4 ,
"author" : "Guest" ,
"text" : "Free. Without SMS, about react, come in - https: //maxpfrontend.ru" ,
"bigText" :
"There is also a VK group, a telegram and a youtube channel! All infa on the site, not advertising!"
}
]

Total : our *App.js is* smart:

src / App.js

```
import React from 'react'
import {Add} from './components/Add'
import {News} from './components/News'
import newsData from './data/newsData' // import by default
import './App.css'
class App extends React . Component {
state = {
news: newsData,
}
handleAddNews = data => {
const nextNews = [data, ... this.state.news]
this .setState ({news: nextNews})
}
render () {
return (
<React.Fragment>
<Add onAddNews = {this.handleAddNews} />
<h3> News </h3>
<News data = {this.state.news} />
</React.Fragment>
)
}
}
export default App
```

Total: we did not tidy up badly, we figured out the imports. Read App.js now
more conveniently, each component lives in a separate file.
There are several approaches to organizing files in large projects, we just did
the first step in this direction.
Source code .

Asynchronous requests

We still don't need redux, nothing like that.

The CRA is designed in such a way that if you put something in the public directory, it will be

available along the way:

http: // localhost: 3000 / directory-name / file-name (but without the word public in the path)

Move our news json to *src / public / data / newsData.json*

Now it can be opened with a GET request to localhost: 3000 / data / newsData.json

Of course, at the same time, the import in *App.js broke* (since such a file, according to the old

no way):

Since we have access to the file via a GET request, we can request it.

"Let's imagine the problem" (c)

We have data on the server (news in json), we need to request it and display it in

list. While the request is being executed, we want to show the user the inscription: "Loading ..."

instead of a news list so he doesn't get nervous. When the news is loaded - we want

display them as before.

What's new in this challenge:

how to make an asynchronous request (the question is not about react) [1];

where to make an asynchronous request (about react) [2];

[1] - this is a question about native js. We will make the request using fetch...

[2] - request for data should start in *componentDidMount*

Let's start by preparing the "state" and template.

src / App.js

```
import React from 'react'
import {Add} from './components/Add'
import {News} from './components/News'
// removed import of newsData
import './App.css'
class App extends React . Component {
state = {
news: null , // was newsData
isLoading: false , // status for manipulation by the "preloader" ("Loading ..." in our
luchae)
}
...
}
export default App
```

At the moment our application is not working, but we have prepared some important

of things:

firstly, we can say based on the data in newsData:

if newsData is null :

if isLoading: false , then the data has not been loaded yet, or

An error has occurred;

if isLoading: true - data is still being loaded

if newsData: [] (empty array) - then there is no news;

if `newsData: [data about news] - then there are news and they are loaded;

In react applications, it all starts with the presentation (description) of the data. Draw in

head or on a piece of paper, since based on such a cheat sheet, it will not be difficult for us

make a template.

Let's start by writing expressions for the template. First:

{Array.isArray (news) && <News data = {news} />}

That is, we check if there is an array in this.state.news - then draw the news component,

he already knows how to draw "no news" or a news list.

IsArray Documentation (MDN)

Second condition:

{isLoading && <p> Loading ... </p>}

Let's style all this in the component:

src / App.js

```
class App extends React . Component {
state = {
news: null ,
isLoading: false ,
}
handleAddNews = data => {
const nextNews = [data, ... this.state.news]
this .setState ({news: nextNews})
}
render () {
const {news, isLoading} = this .state // everything you need was taken from state
return (
<React.Fragment>
<Add onAddNews = {this.handleAddNews} />
<h3> News </h3>
{isLoading && <p> Loading ... </p>}
{Array.isArray (news) && <News data = {news} />}
</React.Fragment>
)
}
}
```

All that remains is to make the asynchronous call and set the correct state.

Remember, we once described with you that the number of news displays numbers in

depending on the data and when they began to add news - we do not this place at all

touched, but the counter worked correctly. This is a **declarative** approach. So it is now -

we, due to the fact that I see the whole picture, described the template and how to behave, and

We will resolve the state at the last step. This trick may not be available.

you have some time while you are learning, so write the code as it is convenient,

for example do something step by step and fight mistakes, the main thing is practice.

Let's go back to the code and make a fetch request + console.log'and. As I said, the request for

data will be done at the moment when the component is already mounted (that is

appeared on the page, that is, we need a lifecycle method - componentDidMount):

src / App.js

```
class App extends React . Component {
...
componentDidMount () {
fetch ( 'http: // localhost: 3000 / data / newsData.json' )
.then (response => {
return response.json ()
})
.then (data => {
console .log ( this )
console .log ( 'data arrived' , data)
})
}
...
}
```

Look in the network, everything works:

Let's take a look at the console and see that since we are using arrow functions, we are not

lost this .

I won't talk about how promise works, but if you have questions, here my favorite materials:

Promise (Cantor)

We have problems with promises (translation of the article on habr)

The lesson comes to its logical conclusion. It remains only to update correctly
component state.

Task : before the request - do isLoading: true, after the request is completed - update
isLoading: false , and put data from the server in news .
(since the solution is in a couple of lines, I will indent. I really want you to try
yourself)

... ...

Solution :
src / App.js

```
...
componentDidMount () {
// set isLoading true,
// that is, the request for data has started
// in fact it will start on the line with fetch,
// but to go from one line to another
// milliseconds will pass
this .setState ({isLoading: true })
fetch ( 'http: // localhost: 3000 / data / newsData.json' )
.then (response => {
return response.json ()
})
.then (data => {
// request completed successfully,
// do isLoading: false
// put the received data in news
this .setState ({isLoading: false , news: data})
})
}
...
```

Interestingly, everything works for us again. We did not touch the
<News /> component , since
again we just changed the "data source".
Since the request for data occurs on localhost, the data arrives instantly.
Let's artificially slow down this moment to see how they "load".
Let's add a timeout, of course.

src / App.js

```
...
componentDidMount () {
this .setState ({isLoading: true })
fetch ( 'http: // localhost: 3000 / data / newsData.json' )
.then (response => {
return response.json ()
})
.then (data => {
setTimeout (() => { // added a delay
this .setState ({isLoading: false , news: data})
}, 3000 ) // in three seconds
})
}
...
```

Wait three seconds and see the news list appear. And what you want note - again, React helps us. The state has changed -> render was called. No
additional manipulations;)
And no Redux / Mobx or anything else. The problem was solved without the "game" in the form of a heap of libraries,
which are not relevant here. Congratulations.
Total : we learned how to execute asynchronous requests and show the preloader.
Source code .

Making a spam filter

It remains for me to highlight the moment of data update. Previously, processing took place in
componentWillReceiveProps , and now in getDervidedStateFromProps (also static).
To do this, I had to invent a problem that is actually solved at the moment
validating news on the backend. But let's say our backend is very busy, and
the manager says - please do it somehow, then we'll finish it (aha!).
Task: if the user, in the added news in bigText, entered 'pubg' - we will
mark such news as SPAM (that is, cut out everything in bigText and insert
line "SPAM").
As follows:

ps i don't mind pubg :) just keep the balance between relaxation and development.

ComponentWillReceiveProps (CWRP)

Let's start with the old lifecycle method (
componentWillReceiveProps),
which will be supported until React version 17. We need to know this because
a lot (a lot) of code has already been written and you will probably get such a project.
src / components / News.js

```
class News extends React . Component {
componentWillReceiveProps (nextProps) {
console .log ({nextProps})
console .log ({oldProps: this .props})
}
...
}
...
export {News}
```

Let's digress for a second and fix the old mistake - in the <Add
/> next to the button, make the text "Add news" instead of "Show Alert".
Let's continue: CWRP takes "future props" in the first argument, so we can
run through them, find news with a "pubg" fragment, if any, and mark it
as "SPAM".
One BUT, since we want to change something, it means that our component has
state! **I draw your attention** : this task is now being solved not optimal
way, we just learn the following points:
how to make state based on props?
how to change state based on newly arrived props?
src / components / News.js

```
...
class News extends React.Component {
state = { // created state
filteredNews: this .props.data,
}
componentWillReceiveProps (nextProps) {
console .log ({nextProps})
console .log ({oldProps: this .props})
}
renderNews = () => {
const {filteredNews} = this .state // use state
let newsTemplate = null
if (filteredNews.length) { // everywhere data is replaced with filteredNews
newsTemplate = filteredNews.map ( function ( item ) {
return <Article key = {item.id} data = {item} />
})
} else {
newsTemplate = <p> Sorry, no news </p>
```

```
}
return newsTemplate
}
render () {
const {filteredNews} = this.state // Similarly, use the state
return (
<div className = "news" >
{this.renderNews ()}
{filteredNews.length? (
<strong className = {'news__count'} >
Total News: {filteredNews.length}
</strong>
): null}
</div>
)
}
}
...
```

There are few changes, just go over the file carefully - now the data
we take from filteredNews, but at the same time they initially come
to us in props (therefore
propTypes left unchanged).
Within *CWRP,* it is safe to use *setState* as it will not result in
additional (unnecessary) redrawing.
src / components / News.js

```
componentWillReceiveProps (nextProps) {
let nextFilteredNews = [... nextProps.data]
nextFilteredNews.forEach ((item, index) => {
if (item.bigText.toLowerCase (). indexOf ( 'pubg' )! == -1 ) {
item.bigText = 'SPAM'
}
})
this .setState ({filteredNews: nextFilteredNews})
}
```

There is nothing unusual in this snippet, for those who are in the
basics (I understand that
the phrase "know the basics" has set the teeth on edge, but you really
need to know them).
In nextFilteredNews cloned the entire array of news from "the future" props
then
ran through it, in the if found out if there is pubg in the text entered in
bigText, and if
yes, replaced with "SPAM".
For those with spaces:
toLowerCase (MDN)
indexOf (MDN)

Total :
learned to create *state* based on *props* ;
learned how to update *state* based on new *props* without unnecessary
redrawing;

static getDerivedStateFromProps

Method signature: static getDerivedStateFromProps (props, state) and documentation, at
which describes that this method is needed for very rare cases. Ourselves
have invented a problem and limitations for the solution, so it will be useful to us.
This lifecycle method is generally similar to *CWRP* , but there are differences:
since the method is static - there is no access to this
the new state should be returned from the method or null if there are no "updates"
planned.
for the first render (*initial render*) - also called
One of the best ways to understand what's going on is console.log
src / components / News.js

```
...
static getDerivedStateFromProps (props, state) {
console .log (props)
console .log (state)
return {
filteredNews: props.data,
}
}
// remove componentWillReceiveProps
...
```

Try to add news.
Let's restore the code that was in *CWRP* , but for
getDerivedStateFromProps (*gDSFR*)
src / components / News.js

```
static getDerivedStateFromProps (props, state) {
let nextFilteredNews = [... props.data] // was nextProps - renamed
nextFilteredNews.forEach ((item, index) => {
if (item.bigText.toLowerCase (). indexOf ( 'pubg' )! == -1 ) {
item.bigText = 'SPAM'
}
})
return { // return a new state
filteredNews: nextFilteredNews,
}
}
```

Refactor

Throughout the tutorial, I taught you to think about data, and then in CWP and gDSFR I took and

made of figuratively *stateless* (although he was through the *class* - he did not have a state)

component - *statefull* . This was done for ease of explanation.

See if we roll back our <News /> two lessons back (when the component just

received props), then we can use gDSFR in <App /> and "cut spam" there.

Thus, we would again solve the problem without changing the stateless component.

It was: the <News /> component was able to display data. Now: component <News />

can display data and mark spam.

Task : process data in <App /> , return <News /> to the previous "dumb" lifestyle.

Hint : you can easily do whatever you need to do in <App /> , since we only

that they worked out this technique.

Hint : in <App />, news is in *state* , not in *props* .

Let me remind you what <News /> looked like :

src / components / News.js

```
import React from 'react'
import PropTypes from 'prop-types'
import {Article} from './Article'
class News extends React . Component {
renderNews = () => {
const {data} = this .props
let newsTemplate = null
if (data.length) {
newsTemplate = data.map ( function ( item ) {
return <Article key = {item.id} data = {item} />
})
} else {
newsTemplate = <p> Sorry, no news </p>
}
return newsTemplate
}
render () {
const {data} = this.props
return (
<div className = "news" >
{this.renderNews ()}
{data.length? (
<strong className = {'news__count'} >
Total news: {data.length}
</strong>
): null}
</div>
)
}
```

```
}
News.propTypes = {
data: PropTypes.array.isRequired,
}
export {News}
```

Decision

Complete component code <App />
src / App.js

```
import React from 'react'
import {Add} from './components/Add'
import {News} from './components/News'
import './App.css'
class App extends React . Component {
state = {
news: null ,
isLoading: false ,
}
static getDerivedStateFromProps (props, state) {
let nextFilteredNews
// look at state.news (previously looked at props)
// and check not to clone null
// for example, at the time of the first rendering
if ( Array .isArray (state.news)) {
nextFilteredNews = [... state.news]
nextFilteredNews.forEach ((item, index) => {
if (item.bigText.toLowerCase (). indexOf ( 'pubg' )! == -1 ) {
item.bigText = 'SPAM'
}
})
return {
filteredNews: nextFilteredNews,
}
}
return null
}
componentDidMount () {
this .setState ({isLoading: true })
fetch ( 'http: // localhost: 3000 / data / newsData.json' )
.then (response => {
return response.json ()
})
.then (data => {
setTimeout (() => {
this .setState ({isLoading: false , news: data})
}, 1000 ) // changed the timer to 1000 so as not to wait long
})
}
handleAddNews = data => {
const nextNews = [data, ... this.state.news]
this .setState ({news: nextNews})
}
render () {
const {news, isLoading} = this .state
return (
<React.Fragment>
<Add onAddNews = {this.handleAddNews} />
<h3> News </h3>
{isLoading && <p> Loading ... </p>}
{Array.isArray (news) && <News data = {news} />}
</React.Fragment>
)
}
```

```
}
export default App
```

Printed in Great Britain
by Amazon

```
}
export default App
```

Printed in Great Britain
by Amazon